CHILDREN'S AUTHORS

L. FRANK BAUM

Jill C. Wheeler

Checkerboard
Library

An Imprint of Abdo Publishing
www.abdopublishing.com

www.abdopublishing.com

Published by Abdo Publishing, a division of ABDO, PO Box 398166, Minneapolis, Minnesota 55439. Copyright © 2015 by Abdo Consulting Group, Inc. International copyrights reserved in all countries. No part of this book may be reproduced in any form without written permission from the publisher. Checkerboard Library™ is a trademark and logo of Abdo Publishing.

Printed in the United States of America, North Mankato, Minnesota.
102014
012015

THIS BOOK CONTAINS RECYCLED MATERIALS

Cover Photo: AP Images
Interior Photos: Alamy pp. 13, 14, 20; AP Images pp. 5, 15, 17; Corbis p. 9; Glow Images p. 19; iStockphoto p. 7; WikiCommons pp. 6, 8, 11, 12

Series Coordinator: Bridget O'Brien
Editors: Rochelle Baltzer, Megan M. Gunderson
Art Direction: Neil Klinepier

Library of Congress Cataloging-in-Publication Data

Wheeler, Jill C., 1964-
  L. Frank Baum / Jill C. Wheeler.
      pages cm. -- (Children's Authors)
  Includes bibliographical references and index.
  ISBN 978-1-62403-665-1
1. Baum, L. Frank (Lyman Frank), 1856-1919--Juvenile literature. 2. Authors, American--20th century--Biography--Juvenile literature. 3. Children's stories--Authorship--Juvenile literature. I. Title.
  PS3503.A923Z93 2015
  813'.4--dc23
  [B]
                          2014025371

CONTENTS

THE MAN BEHIND THE CURTAIN

L. Frank Baum is best known as the author of *The Wonderful Wizard of Oz*. The book is one of the most popular pieces of children's literature ever written. It inspired 13 **sequels** by Baum as well as books by other writers.

Baum was born into a wealthy family. However, **bankruptcy** followed him throughout his life. He was still penning novels as he grew older. He wanted to make sure his family would have money when he was gone.

Though Baum is tightly tied to *Oz*, he wrote many other works. He is the author of nine additional fantasy novels. He also wrote newspaper and magazine articles as well as plays and musicals. Over the years he tried acting, sales, and even **breeding** exotic chickens. Yet he always returned to writing.

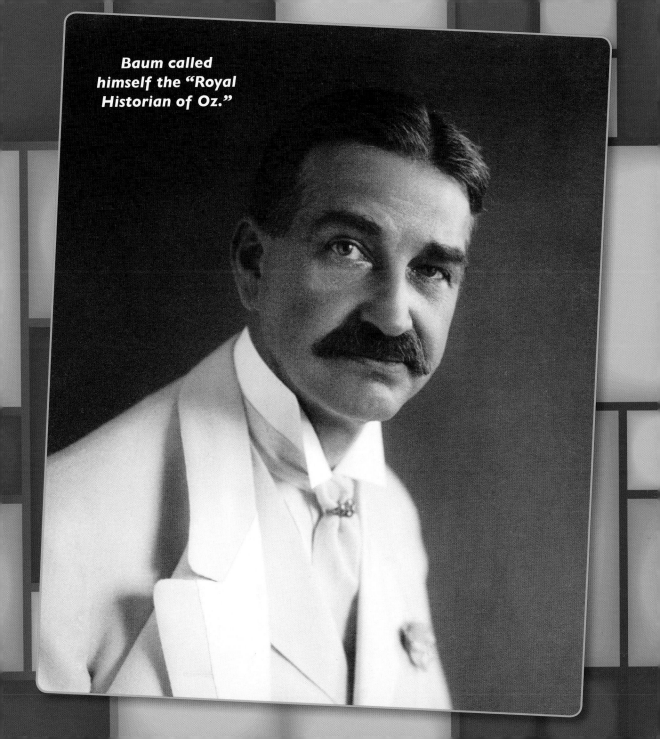

Baum called himself the "Royal Historian of Oz."

A Great Surprise

Lyman Frank Baum was born on May 15, 1856, in Chittenango, New York. He was named after an uncle, but he never liked his first name. He preferred to go by Frank.

Frank later wrote his books on a typewriter using only two fingers!

Frank's parents were Benjamin Baum and Cynthia Stanton Baum. Benjamin was a barrel factory owner. He also made a fortune in the oil business in Pennsylvania.

The Baums had nine children. Five survived to adulthood. Of the surviving **siblings**, Frank's older sisters were Harriet and Mary, and his older brother was Benjamin. His younger brother was Henry.

Frank was born with a heart condition called **angina pectoris**. Because of this, he was not allowed to play rough with other children. He was educated by private tutors at the family's Rose Lawn estate.

When Frank was 12, his parents sent him to Peekskill Academy. This was a military school in New York. Frank hated it! He only spent two years there before going home.

When Frank returned home, his father surprised him with a present. It was a **printing press**. Frank created a neighborhood newspaper called the *Rose Lawn Home Journal* and a literary magazine called the *Empire*. He wrote about stamp collecting and chicken **breeding**.

A printing press Frank might have used when working on his newspaper

ACTING

Frank's father was wealthy. Fortunately for Frank, this meant he could try a lot of jobs without having to worry about money. For a time, Frank was a salesman for his father. He also started a newspaper called *The New Era*. However, nothing stuck.

Frank performed in The Maid of Arran under the name Louis F. Baum

Frank acted for a while in his teens. When he was 23, he joined Albert M. Palmer's Union Square Theatre. He performed under the stage names of Louis F. Baum and George Brooks. His biggest success was acting in a play he had written called *The Maid of Arran*. The show was a surprise hit.

While he was writing *The Maid*, Frank met the young woman he would marry. Maud Gage was the daughter of a prominent **suffragette**, Matilda Gage. Maud and Frank were married in November 1882.

Frank stopped acting when Maud became **pregnant** with their first son. He wrote more plays in his spare time, but none of them were **produced**. He also worked for his family's oil business after his father died in 1887. Unfortunately, the company went **bankrupt** later that year. Frank was in need of a new start.

At first, Matilda Gage (above) did not approve of Frank. But Maud's insistence changed her mind.

DAKOTA TERRITORY

The growing Baum family headed to what is now North and South Dakota. At the time, it was called Dakota Territory. Gold had been found there. Many people wanted to live there and become wealthy. Baum, his wife, and their two sons moved to Aberdeen in what is now South Dakota.

In Aberdeen, Baum ran a store called Baum's Bazaar. The town gave the growing family a newfound social life, and everything was looking up. The couple welcomed their third son in 1889.

However, the good times did not last. After two years of failed crops, local farmers could no longer afford to buy things at Baum's Bazaar. The store failed. Baum went back to writing once again. He worked at the *Aberdeen Saturday Pioneer*. He did most of the writing and printing for the weekly paper.

Baum's Bazaar

The *Pioneer* covered many topics, including weddings, **suffragettes**, and wars. Baum also wrote about Native Americans. Today, those articles would be considered offensive. In 2006, his great-great-grandson apologized for the remarks.

Bad news hit the Baum family again in 1891. The newspaper declared **bankruptcy**, and Baum lost his job. Now with four sons to support, Baum moved his family to Chicago, Illinois.

Story Time

In Chicago, Baum worked as a reporter for the *Evening Post*. But, he did not make as much money as he needed. So, he took another job as a traveling glassware salesman. Baum did very well at sales. He even suggested ways to improve window displays as he went from store to store.

Baum's house in Chicago

At home in the evenings, Baum weaved tales for his sons, Frank, Robert, Harry, and Kenneth. He wanted to create a new fairy tale for American children. He felt some well-known fairy tales were too focused on moral teachings. Instead, he wanted his stories to encourage young people to be self-reliant and positive and to value their families.

Baum's mother-in-law realized he was a natural storyteller. She encouraged him to write down some of his stories. Baum did. He published *Mother Goose in Prose* in 1897.

Mother Goose in Prose was such a success that Baum was able to quit being a salesman. He used his sales experience to write and publish a magazine called the *Show Window*. It taught store owners how to make their windows more appealing to customers.

For his next project, Baum worked with a friend, artist William Denslow. They created *Father Goose, His Book*. The book was published in 1899. It became the best-selling children's book of the year. It had color illustrations, which was rare at the time.

While working as a traveling salesman, Baum created a man made of tin for a window display. This inspired one of Baum's most famous characters!

On to Oz

The original cover of The Wonderful Wizard of Oz

With their last book a success, Baum and Denslow worked together again to bring life to another of Baum's fairy tales. Baum was known for his stories. The neighborhood children would come to his house to hear them. But there was something different about this new story.

As Baum was spinning his tale, a great idea took over. He sent the children away and began writing. He wrote on any piece of paper he could find, including envelopes! His new story was about a young girl and her adventures in a magical land called Oz.

Denslow drew more than 100 illustrations to go with the story. Originally, they wanted to call it *The Emerald City*. But, there is a **superstition** in the publishing world. It said that any book with a jewel in the title would fail. The publisher decided *The Wonderful Wizard of Oz* would do just fine.

Oz became the best-selling children's book of the year in 1900. That Christmas, Baum picked up a check from his publisher for some of the money he earned from *Oz*. Later, Maud asked how much he had made. He handed the check to his wife, who had to hold herself up. She couldn't believe how much money he had made!

There were not many movies in the early 1900s. Instead, books often were made into plays. In 1902, Baum's book was made into a musical called *The Wizard of Oz*. It had the hit song of the season with "When You Love, Love, Love." And audiences loved the play. It had 293 performances and ran for nine years.

A poster for the 1902 musical **The Wizard of Oz**

Only the Beginning

Baum continued to write even as the original *Oz* was performed on stage each night. He wrote more children's books, such as *Dot and Tot of Merryland* and *The Master Key: An Electrical Fairy Tale*. However, none of the other books ever came close to *Oz's* popularity or earned as much money.

Instead, Baum received hundreds of letters from children begging for more stories from Oz. He promised one fan that when he received more than 1,000 letters, he would write again about the fantastical world.

Eventually, Baum received more than 1,000 letters. He kept his promise, too. *The Marvelous Land of Oz* was published in 1904. Dorothy was not in it. But, audiences loved Tip, Saw-Horse, Woggle-Bug, and the other new characters.

Now that Baum was wealthy because of his Oz books, he and his family began to travel. He also continued to write. This time, he branched out from children's books. *The Fate of a Crown* was an adult novel. *Aunt Jane's Nieces* was a series of books for teenage girls. In 1906, Baum went back to writing for children with *John Dough and the Cherub*.

Still, Baum refused to leave Oz totally behind. He wrote *Ozma of Oz* and then *Dorothy and the Wizard in Oz.* He even worked on another stage version of the Oz story. It was expensive. So, he wrote more Oz books to pay the bills.

Baum starred in the new stage version of the Oz story. It was called **Fairylogue and the Radio-Plays.**

OFF TO HOLLYWOOD

By 1910, *The Road to Oz* and *The Emerald City of Oz* were published. Baum moved his family to Hollywood, California, to a new home he named Ozcot. Sadly, even two more books could not help his financial situation. He was forced to declare **bankruptcy** in 1911.

Baum turned to a new form of entertainment, movies. He created the Oz Film Manufacturing Company. His films were not successful. But while filming, Baum got ideas for a new book. *The Scarecrow of Oz* sold well, but not well enough to keep the movie studio open. So, Baum sold it to Universal Studios.

By 1914, Baum's health was declining. He had to stop writing. When he began again two years later, he wrote *Rinkitink in Oz* and *The Lost Princess of Oz*. He also continued writing *The Magic of Oz* and *Glinda of Oz*. He knew that if he died, his family could publish these books and make money. He hid them in a safety deposit box.

The original cover of The Emerald City of Oz

THE EMERALD CITY
of OZ

ILLUSTRATED
by Jno·R·Neill

by L·Frank Baum

In 1918, Baum had an operation to remove his gallbladder. This kept him in bed, but he continued to write. He wrote *The Tin Woodman of Oz* and later prepared *The Magic of Oz* for publication. While taking notes for his next book, Baum slipped into a coma. He died on May 6, 1919, with Maud by his side.

The Magic of Oz and *Glinda of Oz* were published shortly after Baum's death. The Oz **phenomenon** continued, with books written by other authors. Another movie was released in 1925. The most famous version, starring Judy Garland, was released in 1939.

The Oz books are still sold everywhere. Baum once said he "longed to write a great novel that should win [him] fame." It is safe to say that he successfully reached his goal.

The Wizard of Oz, the 1939 movie based on Baum's book, was nominated for five Academy Awards and won two. It is known for its special use of color to help tell the story.

GLOSSARY

angina pectoris (an-JIH-nuh PEK-tuh-ruhs) - a condition where a person's heart doesn't get enough oxygen. It causes chest pains.

bankruptcy - the state of having been legally declared unable to pay a debt.

breed - a group of animals sharing the same ancestors and appearance. A breeder is a person who raises animals. Raising animals is often called breeding them.

phenomenon (fi-NAH-muh-nahn) - a fact or event that is rare or extraordinary.

pregnant - having one or more babies growing within the body.

printing press - a machine that prints books, magazines, and newspapers, usually in large numbers.

produce - to oversee the making of a movie, a play, an album, or a radio or television show.

sequel (SEE-kwuhl) - a book, movie, or other work that continues the story begun in a preceding one.

sibling - a brother or a sister.

suffragette (suh-frih-JEHT) - a woman who worked to get women the right to vote.

superstition - a belief that some action not connected to a future event can influence the outcome of the event.

WEBSITES

To learn more about Children's Authors,
visit **booklinks.abdopublishing.com**. These links are routinely
monitored and updated to provide the most current information available.

INDEX

J
B
Baum
W

Wheeler, Jill C.,
1964-   author.

L. Frank Baum.

DATE			

10|16-2(3|16)